COLLECTED POEMS

Michael Scott

Fisher King Publishing

Collected Poems
Copyright © Michael Scott 2013
ISBN 978-1-906377-61-8

Fisher King Publishing Ltd
The Studio
Arthington Lane
Pool-in-Wharfedale
LS21 1JZ
England

Cover painting by Michael Scott

Collected Poems

Poetry should speak for itself. But a little explanation may be appropriate.

In this book you'll find the poems are broken up into sub-sections which give some indication of their provenance. They are as follows –

Signs of Life
These were early poems in which I was trying to find my poetic language and understand my existence.

Personal Notes
Here you will find poems which cover a range of family and other similar matters.

Pagan Encounters
Poems purely about mystical subjects.

Poems of Redemption
These pieces refer to spiritual concepts.

Sacred Songs
A collection that project a range of introspective or philosophical ideas.

Evening Music
Every piece here, on specified subjects, was written for meetings of a poetry group.

CONTENTS

Pagan Encounters

Poems of Redemption

Sacred Songs

Evening Music

Signs of Life

Howl at Night

I pull my guilt up to my chin
And curse myself to sleep
The morning cannot keep away
My dreams are cold and deep
The silly dawn will cry about
The stars sit tight and grin
A memory will have its day
Old virtue breeds new sin.

Eyes of the Dead

Red remembrances staring on stone in the square
Make no difference. Nor comfort for arthritic bone;
We decay as we stand and regret the dead young
Who were sacrificed splendidly, dying so soon
In the blood and the mud of a black afternoon.

A Straw too Few

My soul runs cool
The night blows light,
Waters play a likely tune.
Wishes jump across the gap
Terrors heap about and wait;
The sun is shining now
And roses shout their due,
White music drowns the wind
But pity picks a straw too few
To save itself and stay.
Eyes fill a frozen stream
And all the world is
Hot with hateful laughter

Tom Tiddler's Ground

There can be no mistake, where errors heap
To make this total desert; only sleep.
Great meanings blossomed sweet
In that rich unknowing;
Now fool and flowers meet
Their dead hopes - vowing
Lost love - receive defeat
And a fine fragrance no-one else can keep.

So this is my estate: the middle land
And what is cultivated? Shifting sand.
My green has been burnt white,
Impertinences blackened
One cold hard-hurting night:
The death line - slackened
From negligence - drew tight
And I am stretched across a signless strand

Spring

Stilted lambs with windmill tails
Make a trembling fuss of being
Woollen grasshoppers.
Yellow yawning crocuses
Stretch and break their pretty necks in
Morning sunshine. Poplars:
Elderly, respectable, grey
Eminences, catch a greenish
Fever, happily.

Sufficient unto thy Day

One flesh enduring one more unexpected summer
Loves everything it cannot keep;
The flower we picked for reference is pressed between us
Identified and dried.
But innocence takes time to grow. And that poor primrose
Laid down its life to make us weep;
To outstare panic in the one-way window,
And know we can consume our pride

Communicating Door

Only faces recognised between us
And insanity. If eyes and mouths made
Patterns homogeneous like daisies'
Blank expressions, then would you and I be
Mirrors without love or hate. And losing
Our identities would know our being;
Understand the flowers' quiet dying
And, anonymous, become the other.

Reference-point

Tell me how to speak to you,
Let you know what I have seen
Through the space where I was brave
And when I had a longer day.

Calculate my measurements.
Catch me in a jam-jar tight;
Label it with love, my love,
To show what I have not become.

Wistful Thinking

I would rather dream of long and lovely summer days
As a way of waiting while the time is ticking out,
Put the shivering consciousness to warm, out in the sun;
Entertain the sadly breaking heart with tricks
Picked up in sheltered places where the men
With peaceful faces sit and smile:
I would rather dream.
But I am tall and I must try to pick the fruit;
I must stretch upon my toes to reach the tree.
I must look into the eagle's angry nest;
Put my hand into the fire,
Still I listen for the crying of the dying things,
Take upon myself their unbelievable mortality:
For happiness is impropriety in this, a proper world.

Memory Lane

Sharply seeing sunning marigolds today,
Yellow and orange marigolds,
Yellow and orange and yellow marigolds,
Sunstricken marigolds;
I was twenty years ago today,
Summering again some precious pains.

Then the melting of the crystal code
Breaking the case enclosing golden horrors
Hanging like bats; disturbed by the light,
Shrieking silently, flying to the yellow sun
Orange and yellow light
Orange and yellow and orange sun.

A Little Knowledge

As I laughed and cried and loved
His bright eyes
A little bird told me
All that he knew
All that he knew about being alive
For a time
In the snows
And the summers;
All that he knew about fighting
And fear, and the dying
That comes with the searching
And working:
The claws and
The jaws and
The sky and the wind and
The leaves.
All that he knew.
All that I know.

Halcyon Summer

As this surprising sun lays his rays upon us
Each dedicated fool defies his lord
And mocks his own deceitful dilgence:
Such is the killing of a king.
Friends and fruit are not so passionately preserved
But eaten fresh and ripe - with cream -
You and I, before the midnight snow begins
Will love a kingfisher inside our summer dream.

Poor Sparrow

Feathers seem to grow in tarmac
As the God is snugly in His heaven.
My sorrowing for sparrow's fall
Is great enough for godless places.
Your driving killed him acrobatically:
Little fool behaved as if he were the only one
Using your robbing highway, and he paid for it,
God served him right for careless hopping in your right of way.

Love Offering

Here is a little pain for you to share
To have, to hold, to keep me company.
Can you feel it? Are we a pair? Are you sure it is
My tiny agony you feel.
You would not be so blind and cruel
To feel a misery of your own, and fail
In my pale grey dawn of misery.
I wish I could be sure your sympathy
Was externally directed,
Aimed at me
And not at your own and undeserving personality.

Adjustment

What little victory this
What monstrous cost
To be my own beginning
So many fine young
Hours were lost
Upon this wasteful winning

Truly I say and
Never know I lie
Believing no believing
Not seeing through
This empty eye
That time is always leaving

I am only chaos
Sensitised
Ask atoms their intention
This silence must be
Analysed to find
No destination

Pneumania

Beating, pumping, thumping, jungle-stomping;
Heart on ear-drums hops a hopeless polka.
Silence. Has it stopped - at last? No fear. No sweat!
Drifting; swimming. Quiet. Then a pain. At first a presence.
Then a giant, detaches from the hollow body,
Swoops, clamps itself across the throat. Vicious.
Clumsy vampire: teeth grate upon mistaken swallowing.
Foolish chest contracts to cough, a star explodes across
That swollen space: the room inside the head.
Nostrils, eyelids, cheekbones grow, expand, collapse,
Deliquescent face flows down into a pillow's apathy.
Brain coagulates inside its pan; is turned; is terrorised:
Seeing antibodies prosper, multiply, riding high,
Remembers other vandalising plasms, recognises murderous intent.
Victim! Patient! Fix a bayonet! Combat will be intimate.
Also decisive. Fear is normal. Only fools are brave.
Coward cheats. Aims artillery upon virus cavalry.
Tetracycline holocaust carbonises chivalry.

Let the Music Choose

Winter kill comes long too late for jockey corpse,
Riding cocky, horsey; happy holiday apocalypse;
Nodding, winking, extra-loving; bleakly bright.
Fool, she, tries to be, a guilty party, to adultery
With spring, with celandines, with buzzing copulatory
Blue, bottled, potty diptera; blue-tittery, or
Gold-finchery, or all the blue and black winged birdery.
Lady, lady, be contrary; let the past go by,
Look your tinted destiny in its wrinkled eye.
Sing, cry, dance, sigh: skeletal butterfly.
Winter kill comes long too late for jockey corpse.
Let the music choose the time for you to die.
When it stops.That is.

Boar Hunt

In the forest of his nature
The creature hears and waits;
Comprehends the messages of destiny,
Intuitively hates
This death intruding
On his familial land,
Suddenly convulses in
Advance of meeting killing hand,
Plunges, now away, now towards
The pack of dogs, of men.
His own tribe free, away:
His rage, his fear, his rage again
Hold him to this place, deliver him
To the lance, scream his screams.
He dies within his fear, inside his rage:
Down blood streams.
In the forest of his nature
The creature's fear is dead.
In the forest of his nature
The blades of grass are red.

Personal Notes

Mother

Having wept a sea of salt and vinegar, my heart sings

Her praises. My bird-mind cocks his eye at me and asks, 'What of it?'

That struggling, striving, often frantic hen fed my craw and cleaned my nest.

If I could stand separate from my pride, my cock's comb, a moment

I could see the bird-bright vigilance of her brooding care and find

Her flying soul alongside mine, as it always was and always will.

As any bird she could only do so much, no more, no less, before

Her body and her spirit perished, broken by the indifferent machinery

That snaps and tears its way towards me also and to everything and all

The others I love and live beside. So, true, my mother did have limitations.

Hard for chicken-child to bear: a chicken-mother's imperfection.

Chicken-child is perfect - or rather might be – but for chicken-mother's faults?

She had ten, or fifteen, years to make me wonderfully invulnerable, to make

Of me a shining glory? This, I think, she tried to do: fortunately failed.

Fail she might, try she did, and how and who am I to ask

That it should have been otherwise? Why allow the backward glare

Of a fledged fool, seeing weary mother-bird culpable to infinity or more?

Is any new chick free to expect everything, to make a future dossier of fault

To warm itself to its own triumphant dying crash? Let me say, then:

I want none of it. That bird-mother is secure and sitting on her perfect nest.

My Father's House

My father's house is orderly, carefully arranged, neat
Nervous of chaos and failure he arranges where he can
And grumbles when other forces intervene untidily.
He is afraid of tomorrow and puts things ready for it:
His lunchbox, thermos, breakfast plate and cup, set
In line, to save time, to help him face the morning.
But when there is no work for him, he sits and pines
In his tidy house and longs for fearful mornings to come again.

My father's house has a garden that is like his house.
The vegetables are tidy, lawn and hedges well-shaved.
There is a shed in it, with coal, and tools and my bicycle
Which is welcome there, despite its being mine, his gift.
I love his lettuces and carrots and great cold cabbages,
I love his shed and its infinite variety of order;
And around the squares of grass are pale yellow tulips,
Sweet-smelling carnations, stocks and lilies-of-the-valley.

My father's house has anger in it, long silences, loud curses.
He is not enough a king, he is fed but not honoured.
There is pain in him and in his house: he suffers a wound
That may be unimportance, or ignorance, or poverty or shame.
Or maybe it is the endless labour, with no praise or prizes;
And little friendship. He tries to joke, tell stories, even sing
His favourite tunes. But his house returns a hollow ring.
No-one loves him enough to make his heart take wing.

My father's house was a place to get away from, even for him
Not his at all, it was his prison, he had to go there.
He tried to make it home, but it fought him off, a roof
Over his head, a bed under his back, a place to eat.
He'd put the wireless on, the Pirates of Penzance would sing
But his joy was unrequited. He had come from a frugal
Hour in the Lamb Inn, full of bonhomie that soon died.
He'd take me for a walk and he knew he was too lonely.

So I am rebuilding my father's house, now he's long dead.
There are big windows, generous fireplaces, panelled walls;
Thick carpets, enfolding chairs, potted plants, decanters
Of whisky, good wines, fruit, huge soft beds, music machines
Everywhere, the Welcome mat at every door; a warm bathroom,
And lavatories to rest in, central heating, and four assertive cats;
Around the great kitchen blows and flaps the presence of a cook
Who loves my father's table as generously as she loves him.

Around the new house of my father we make a garden such as
Rich men have: skyscraping trees, a lake, an orangery, terraces,
Languid nymphs, Olympic heroes, avenues, temples, bridges
Over a troutful stream, aviaries, orchards, gazebos, conservatories.
Here he walks, smiling, radiant with the mystery of it all
Nothing and everything his, as it always was, a humble man,
Anxious to be entranced. We work together. I show him
My joy in flowers, he holds them to his heart.

So here is my father's kingdom and he at last is king.
I have put him where he needs to be, and his son can become me.
His rule is gentle here, his lightness illuminates the new house
And out across the great garden; and his darkness lies
Safely in hollows and woodlands. My father is master now
Of his domain; firm and certain, the ghost made flesh, spirit
No longer wastes itself in idle rage. My father's new house
Has many mansions, enough for all my fathers and all my kings

My father's house is also big enough for me and all my loves,
My gods and heroes, my fears and dreams. Now I belong
In the house of my father and my fathers and my ancient kings.
I take my leave of the lonely place I made for my orphan self
A bunker in the desert where I have grown old. I walk the long trail
To my father's house; full of music; old, old songs; love
Has been looking for its home for years as long as centuries:
I least expected it might rest within my father's bony arms

And from the safety of their strange embrace I look out again
At a world transformed by an unexpected vantage-point:
I see the one that battled fatherless against the fathers,
That raged kingless against the kings, godless against the gods
And needed too needily the sweet and bitter solace of women.
That poor man had lost his father - mislaid him, rather,
Put him beyond reach for failing to live up to presumptive glory.
Two poor men were now one, living tidily in my father's house.

We are orderly, the rooms are carefully arranged, neat
We are nervous of chaos, fearful of failure, we arrange
Ourselves in our house to keep alien forces away, tomorrow
Makes us anxious; we try to prepare, set ourselves up for it.
Morning comes, we meet in our great kitchen: eggs and bacon,
Toast, coffee, and imaginary cigarette. What shall we do today?
There's nothing to be done. In the new house of my father
We look out at the garden and decide to take each other for a stroll.

(With thanks to Robert Bly's 'Iron John')

Her Death

Such a Sunday: with a brown and blue bright face
Took me to her breast to suckle dry champagne,
While another day lay dying, as I played,
And as the other days were dead already.
When the wine had dried and tears had washed the glass,
A dear day's flesh was cold and solid:
A day that went too quickly and too quietly.
She was the mother of the child I was, and she had died without a word
As I smiled into a Sunday's simpering face.
But the child is also dead and cannot lose.
I have seen the child and mother dead
And there is only time to bleed.

On the Death of My Sister's Cat

Each cat has three forms, a self in triplicate
Always the same parts, different only in degree
From cat to cat; but a balance so delicate
That any cat is unique and also monotonous

In having the habits of its tribe: the cat-collective.
This the first part, the killing, fighting, scratching self,
That yawns, excretes, washes, lifts its tail; reflective
Of the racial catness, the essence as the animal.

Also of the lineage is the luxuriating sycophant
Using its human enemy as lover, converting the
Unpredictable ape into soft affection. This, now arrogant,
Now charming, now foolish, self melts the biped's heart.

When death intervenes, both these selves are mourned:
Once in love, the human takes the animal as it is.
Horror, nausea, exasperation: the creatures, man and cat,
Formed in the crucible of life, living to kill, killing to live,

Man loves beast as he loves himself. Even more the grief:
The loss of charm, of purring, stroking, rubbing self.
In life, the cat could steal our wits; in death, it is the thief
Of peace, of certainty, and makes a dark and lonely space.

More than enough, this: but not yet enough. The third
Self takes, and gives, the most. The hardest to see. The worst to lose.
The spirit of the bird-killer is itself a miraculous bird
That flies and sings in another universe, just within our grasp.

Orchis

I seem to see a simile, the greenish ghost of a smile:
Metaphor-potted, terracottaged prisoner, dying while
Time bled unblessed from my perforated living-style
Orchis came to us in fullest bloom, eager flowers for my love
Long leaves like green straps, springing, trailing, above
Swollen fennel-bases, every blossom was a flying yellow dove.
I watched it die for half a year, slowly; yet faster than me
Orchis made me remember my green youth, it seemed to be
Closer now. And closer still was my mortality.
It's death like mine seemed premature,
The rules: *No Food, No Water*; the book was sure
My love said, 'Break the Rules'; a sort of cure.
Orchis and I were simultaneously then re-potted:
And a place in a limbo, for each, allotted
Together in a greenhouse - we should have rotted.
To my surprise, orchis grew; and so did I.
Years and days of iconoclastic food and drink passed by
For orchis as I willed to hope I'd see it bloom before I'd die
Then, last spring, there sprang a pregnant budding stem
It could not be a flower, the Rules specifically condemn
A food and water diet for man and orchis, especially not for them.
But flower it did: bold yellow flying doves - again
And was it possible to think that love's blithe disdain,
That amiable incoherence, could some degree of life for me regain?
That flower died. A year went by. Another winter came.
Then out of my lethargy, on another day, I see the same
Spring of life in orchis: those flying wings of yellow flame

On the Return of a Cat, or Anyone Else
(The nine ways of going, and returning)

First, the Monster of the Labyrinth calls, and you must go
To take the challenge, to kill the Minotaur. All well and good.
I cannot and would not stop you but here, take the thread,
A golden cord to lead you there and guide you out again.
You must defeat him; I understand the need; and here's the line,
The love-line you will follow when you're ready to return.

Then the treasure: its beauty beckons from a distant place,
Your eyes, your ancient messages, fix upon that far-off joy.
Heaven is anywhere you need to be. So take your trip. Go.
But keep your memory of earth within your heart. And so,
When paradise has given you its fruits, look within and see
This other treasure: a place where you can always safely be.

Thirdly is the path of Other Love, to a different love from me.
I would hold you to me and I would make you free.
With pain and blessing, both, I watch you leave. I see
That to keep you I must lose you and if I then find me
Only then can you return - when you are sure you're free -
This way back, for you, is in this: my own autonomy.

Fourth is the darkness, your old passion for the night
Where you will recombine your being with the forest hunters
And with the wild spirit of your daytime shadow, a journey
Into the Underworld, into a place of fear, of black and blood.
From there, return is difficult. You must remember how to wake.
Remember, there, that you are sleeping, and then the spell can break

Or you may seek the sleep of the sun, the golden dreaming.
The fifth death is enticement of the Yellow God, the shining one;
In his hot glory grow also glorious: Lion, Star, Volcano. Or
Like an emperor, an Aztec king, you look upon yourself supreme.
Escape from this is like a fall, to return you must descend
A thousand steps, down to the damp and shade, and love, and being.

Six is in sensuality, addiction, greed: carnal beatitudes.
Excess enchants, appetite entrances, and satiation disappoints.
You grow fat. Or you grow thin. Gross or spindly, the same thing:
It is death by neglect; the tide of laziness takes all territory
Left undefended. The way back is just a narrow causeway
And you will get across if you start now, if you can run.

The seventh way is the rage for change: haven is trap, trap haven;
Meat is prison, prison meat; it is too hot, too cold, too wet, too dry.
This way is anger, this way is shame, and impatience, and fear,
If it were different, if only it would be otherwise, then you would
Want it different again. To return from this requires an act of grace:
You might have to wait; it might be too late; or you may about-face,

The eighth place of death is the tomb of despair, there's nothing there
But the certainty that nothing is everywhere. There you will sit
Immobile, sad, dejected, not seeing or wanting or loving
Any thing: because there is nothing. To return from there is hard
Even to contemplate, because you cannot even think. To put
One foot upon the path of life you must find love, loving, and love life.

The ninth way, unconsciousness, is a matter of duration and degree.
Generally, you simply wake. Occasionally you leave your present body
And return by finding it again. Once in a lifetime you find another way.
Another body, if available, is ideal, though not essential; you'll see
The possibilities multiply, now your consciousness is free. Of all
The deaths, this one is most misunderstood and easiest reprieved.

Metamorphosis of the Phoenix People

Like the recurrent bird, but frequently and differently,
We give ourselves into the fire, therein are oxidised towards
All-recognition.
Our elements re-arranged, our atoms re-combined
Transmutation of self into self and again into
Self; and soul there grows - from burning to burning
A sight of gold in ashes.
Alchemy was ever more inspired. This empiricism
A deduction from the whole: the burning in the vessel
Frees spirit of intention
Cryptographs broken into Particular Realities
Unpalatable. Nothing nutritious laid until the table
Clears itself of familiar comforts, is polished like glass
Reflecting vanities.
Spirit, enervated by consideration of its own apostasy
Diminishes to candlle-point. the great flame lies down
Flickers out
Now spirit in its death defies ideas of resurrection
Dead spirit is hardly inconvenience, its breath would only
Disturb our sleep
Let it lie there in the vault of false promising
For if it reconstitutes we will burn again, suffer everything
Yet again.
But see: the trees blossom; the birds are nesting there
An older spring insinuates into spirit's form, a slow

Radiance creeps: autonomous, it raises spirit from that
Resting place
And then the rushing heat, that familiar, fearful, heat
Of violent, flaming, wings - we recognise a thousand
Stings
Once more we enter half in bliss the place of metamorphosis.

Love's Choice

I do not choose love: it chooses me: and burns me up
And in that furnace hate and fear are forged, as if desired
Then I burn them up again and new love oozes from the old

I do not search for suffering, it finds me; embraces me.
In its tightening grip I remember nails and thorns
But pain stops, some time, always if compassion flows.

I do not expect friendship, it surprises me; and betrays me,
In the wild, salt, bitter sea the souls freezes over to protect itself
Till, thrown upon the shore, I see my friend grown good and old.

I do not reach for faith; it falls upon me; hurts my head.
In the chase, after the rolling apple, I trip, fall, lose all sense
Except the memory of it, the apple that chose my head.

I do not want God, It wants me - demands, abandons, kills me
Reincarnate me as anything It fancies, I am God's fantasy, I see.
But I have lost the confidence that God's a fantasy for me.

I review my plight, debatable but undeniable, a less unlikely story,
Chosen by love, found by suffering, and surprised by friendship.
Faith falls heavily upon my head and ITGODVOID commandeers me

My fear, my pain, my suffering, are merely raw materials for loving

And into that same pot goes revenge, remorse, broken bones, hypothermia

And, falling down, my human rights, my human wrongs, pride and egomania.

Holy Gender-ation

I half awoke, to absorb the shock, but off
I went again, and there she was again,
But different: now she was absolutely
Complete, bejeweled, beautiful, unneedful
Of anything at all, from me or anyone. I
Swam in my own sea of frustration,
Here was a woman, glorious, exciting, the
Best I had encountered, with this one defect,
She had no needs, none whatever. Thus I
Awoke again, and mulled it over. Here
Was mystery. My dream-woman was, of
All things, perfect, damn it. If she is
My soul, where does that leave me? My
Soul is complete, perfect, fine. all on its own?
Ah, I think: that's the reality; life's work
Is to perfect the soul all right, but not for
Me, as such, whoever I might be. The soul's
Perfection is for Itself? Can that be true?

If true, I thought, it makes all things worse
In the 'Point of Life' department. Or better,
Yet, depending on where I stand. Dream Woman,
Soul or not, is autonomously her own self,
And even if she is just a figment of my
Projection, self-centred fantasy, it makes

No difference: the lesson is diamond-edged,
Hard as nails: my maleness looked for comfort
From femaleness with the soft touch, cool hand
Upon my fevered flesh, that old dream, long
Dead. Then I thought that 'she' was in my head
To make me perfect and I should stand the pain
For my own good sake and maybe also for
The unknown gods as all the doctors say.
And now the story bends and cracks:
If comfort exists, if progress could ever be,
Do not look for it within the Ancient She
Who is frying an altogether private fish.

Is there another theory in the wings
Of this elusive flying fish? If only
One that asks 'why dream this dream'?
I see my mind think that, after all, Ceridwen's Quarry
There's something here for me; if dreams are any
Use, these ladies are here for me even if
They aren't. Why, perhaps, I ought to ask
Do I feel so damned pleased. How is it
That a dream of personal irrelevance could
Make me bubble with a cheerful gas?
Is it possible that in the heart of man, in
The masculine cockpit, there is a truth
Buried and forgotten, to the effect that

I am also autonomous, unneedful, and
Where does that leave soul? I know: men
Try to steal the souls of women, because they
Think they have none of their own, or can't
Be bothered with the endless hard work.

Bigbrain

Bigbrain longs for knowledge of
Itself. Otherwise assumes the worst,
And best, of its own imagination:
True, pending truth, till knowledge comes.
Believes there must be thoughts
That bless the thinker and
Understanding that can elevate
The understanding head.
Bigbrain allows no possibility
Unworthy of a cosmic crochet-needle;
Turning up patterns in the dusty attic,
Searching for significant items, left idle
But useful, somehow, given time
To work it out, where it fits, there
In Bigbrain's attic, the truth appears to lie
And if not truth, maybe beauty. Virtue?
The reward is knowledge. Even bad news
Has its price, or do I mean its own reward?

Pagan Encounters

Inner Children

Like but unlike the children of the fickle goddess
They step into the sunlight of the glade, orphans,
Fourteen years between them, neither dark nor fair,
Not freakish like the other boy, nor pretty either,
Like the other's sister; these are not celestial spawn.
This boy is doubting-mind, this girl's called fearful-heart,
Gifts of despair, unhappiness, if left unappraised
Yet meant to be helpful, this scruffy, waiflike pair
Keeping the hard world in check, as if they really could.
Such unfair burdens for children and I must arise
And free them, take their gifts, make an alchemy
As is intended; so they, girl and boy, are young again.

Ceridwen Creates

The third boy, another myth of rage and alteration,
Becomes the poet, unreal but true in spirit, who
Is chased by the mad goddess, a fairy epic tale
Which bites and chews the mind, and rips and
Shapes the world, as boy and woman tear the veils
Of reason, mind-beings that turn the mind upon itself.
Then I speak the story, pulling it from the dead page,
Prising off the flat words and rounding them on my tongue;
Singing the words, creating bird, fish, beast and grain,
And I am made new, reformed in mind's flesh,
As if the goddess, like crazy Kali, tires of entropy
And turns to her other destiny, making us all one.

Unpredictable Space

This glade, grove, haven, garden, is not what it seems.
Like Ceridwen and the boy-magus Gwion, there is change
In each leaping moment, and haven-heaven takes
On the fleeting image of prison-hell; then back again,
Sometimes gentle, with grass, flowers, water and dryads,
Sometimes fierce, a briar patch, nails not flowers, fire and sulphur.
Or on another day, it is a drama, illusory, all moods and
Space-time warps, or sweetest childhood dream-memories.
Something in the woody nature of the glady grove spells death
As much as life; the passing days and seasons, and the dark
Mystery spread through the stars: this is not safety. Nor yet
So hazardous; just a place of death, life, memory and immediacy.

Caring Nature

Web-weaver, shape-shifter, shaman, writer, painter: Name-
Maker's storming brain scatters my burning ashes over
Fifty fleeting years, a thousand pictures, and ten million words.
Living to create or creating to live; either way the poet's game
Is Eliot's mug's and old as I get the more I play as if
My death, nodding companionably towards me, is woven too
And my life itself a webbed, mind-mapped song of earth.
Now is the giving moment, time to turn again with love
And praise and pity for the holy planet, my only god, spinning
In the sea of space, to this tiny biosphere, my joy and fear,
Taking the treasures of my many years, my offerings, and any
Still to come, and putting them upon the altar in the sacred wood.

Sick Shaman

An invitation: 'Meditate upon Earth and tell about your body';
May I refuse, say I am otherwise engaged, mowing the green?
I know I will not like what is revealed. Seen it before. Well,
Look again. From a new perspective. From inner or outer space.
Oh god-earth, you're suffering more than ever. Still beautiful
In parts, but so much of you is dead or dying, the natural course
Of human occupation. As in my body, so in yours, suffering
The presence of the new ape, the best and worst hominid, you
Have made an Aaron's rod for your own back. I have lived out
My body as it has lived out me. Now that's not to say there
Has not been ecstasy and celebration for us both, descants
Above the threnody, but the ultimate tune is plangent grief.

Divine Soliloquy

It all depends on what you mean by 'prayer' and what god
You think is there and whether listening. We could argue for
Eternity, if it were available, and still not comprehend each
Other. Does god-earth feel or think, do you suppose? Is it not
Merely animated biochemistry? Like you, I feel it would be
A shame if it were so. The buzziness of consciousness alone
Might do quite well for blame and idolatry, if not exactly
Deity, as it is generally promoted. Then the simple art of
Meditation may be an adequate placebo, without divine
Certainty, yet leading to overwhelming answers, a loaded lexicon:
Extirpate the poisoned roots, greed, hatred and delusion, walk peace
As if the god-earth had his ear to the ground beneath your feet.

Beltane Gathering

Or his eye to the keyhole of my life, the transcendent voyeur,
Was he watching, if he exists, his feast of fertility? We made
Beltane again. Out in the world, about in the clanging streets,
Inauspicious buildings, there was no sign of recognition, Paganism
Is as dead as an extinct dormouse. We heard a Sufi accupuncturist
Tell his homilies, the rules by which he played the instrument of
His prescribed existence. We bought a tree, and water-plants, an
Orchid, in a place which could have been a god-earth temple but only
Thrummed to the sound of money. Then, at last, we met them, the few
Disciples of nature assembled beneath a cold, moon-brilliant sky.
The Ceremony shone its light on us and we were whole again. And on the
Same Beltane day, in the sun of the afternoon, a new grove was born.

Earthy Rebellion

Two gargoyles grin upon the Weaving of the Earth: one is scepticism
The other, self-importance. I take the challenge in the spirit of new
Seeing: if Earth can heal Man, can Man heal Earth? And moreover,
Can they recognise the blackness in each other? Yes or no, I hesitate
To heal or be healed, not praying, not knowing outcomes in advance.
But ceremony need not wait upon certainties. The stones, the earth,
The salt, have their own language, and I listen open-eared. The rough
Rock of inheritance holds heavier than the smooth stone of aspiration,
Yet the ordinary awareness has it opposite. The pot of earth tells
Of essence and holiness, the salt speaks of love and life. Then rage
Takes me, tells me further truths. I have played to others' tunes too
Long, The fathers and forefathers have covered my earth in blood.

Naked Mind

Enlightenment is capricious, visiting the mind after closing time.
I've made a hundred trips to the inner grove, unwelcomed, unsafe,
Often, not always, usually. This time it is a closed box of yew.
A maze of yew hedges beyond. Inside the box, I am alone with grass.
This is safety: a closed cell. I jump out of the box like Jack on a
Spring. Then I am in the circle of trees, with water and flowers,
And anyone can invade my space. I cannot be at peace, naked, asleep.
It's no enigma: I have lived my inner being out in the open street,
I invited violation, I had no place to call entirely mine, even and
Especially inside myself. Non-self is the aim of Amida, but even
He needed a home somewhere, as do I, and if others enter, as they
Must, they will now have to wipe their feet and mind their manners.

Antelope

He enters gently, unexpectedly quiet, graceful, toe-tipping
Towards me. I thought he might be a wild boar, maybe a cat
Or a great bird, conventional animals of power. He is large
Though. At least he's big. And his long horns are stiffly sharp.
He is confident, unafraid, as if he knows me from way back.
I put out my hand and touch him. He watches my face with
Black, bottomless eyes, as I feel his muzzle, and the solid
Skull beneath his sand-coloured hide. I am moved to utter
Joy that he should come to me bringing the gift I most desire
The absolute virtue of gentleness, the power that is no power.
I, a hunter by ancestry, try to imagine his world; grazing,
Companionship, sleeping, sudden death, and it is also mine.

Water

Earth is both planet and element, a fusion without confusion;
But water is pure element, even though it almost owns the Earth.
It is my element, in rivers, streams, lakes and garden ponds.
And in a small dish near my face, I feel its molecules bouncing
Up, it has a silent presence, like a beloved friend, and the taste
Upon my tongue is a benediction. Water flows like the metre
Of a poem, or the run of a song, and songs are sung to water.
When I was young, water, or sometimes better, snow, drew me
Into its being. Becks at the sides of fields were gateways to
A magic world. Snow made me wild with desire. The sea made me
Crazy. Nearly killed me sometimes. Then I learned to swim. And
Dive. And once I fished, until I saw the other's pain, and stopped.

Tolerant Spirit

Dreaming life into the Earth, the blue planet, new virtues dawned,
Asking to be heard. Would we, mankind, not multiply nor overlive
Our welcome? Could we tolerate diversity, amongst ourselves, our
Neighbours, give up enmity, smile on gods and no-gods, listen to
Another's language as music? Would strong and weak help each other?
I also dreamed of suffering in those who do not speak at all. Fishes
In the streams and seas, birds and insects in the air, mammals and
Reptiles on the earth, creatures with senses, minds, identities and
Not ours to kill. And trees and flowers and seaweeds and corals
Not resources to be plundered, and if we use them can we be frugal
And considerate? And the earth and water and air: ancient elements
Need us to stay at home, or learn to walk again, and be civilised.

Poems of Redemption

If We became Kind

. . . . if we became kind
To those who come after us, worm or wolf, gnat or eagle, if we
Wanted to reform; a closing gesture, we could end our days
As global cleaners, leaving world nearly as we found it, when
We walked tall and dark out of Africa a piffling million years ago.
Is that what we will do, now? An act of renewal and redemption,
Our humble gift, so that we can die with smiles upon our faces,
The happiest of endings? Why not, a poet wonders, now we've lost
All there was to lose on earth, leave graciously our borrowed empire?

Seed the Planet

Does man-free earth need, deserve, or warrant holy gifts of goodness?
We were never pure enough to make them work anywhere near the letter
So why should wildebeest or alligators or gnats do any better?
Sapiens by name, if not by nature, we never really trusted our intelligence
Enough to make of it a golden mean, too afraid of it, this hardest master.
Too clever by half, too stupid by three-quarters, we spat on our inheritance
And by and large outdid the animals in bestiality. Call it a design-fault
If you will, but we were worse than nothing - a good idea admittedly
But incompetent in execution. However, the technology is there, done
Is the science, and we could seed the planet with intelligence, if that
Made sense. But how to know that? That's the Prince of Denmark's question.
Oh, planet earth, little darling of the universe, would you like to be a prodigy?

At Least We Tried

Oh, sweet, amoral, Nature, innocently savage planet, should we
Ape the blind romantic optimist and try to make you wise and good?
If we could we might but maybe fortunately we certainly cannot.
Mission totally impossible: Nature cannot be converted to love
And kindness, for Nature is mainly made of parasites great and small
Whose ethics are beyond reproach, being entirely absent. How might
Morality have arisen, is there any sign, anywhere, in anything, but us?
Well, of countless kinds, some very few show signs of primitive grace:
Gulls wring grass-stems in preference to each others' necks. Stags battle
Ritualistically. Cats and others cosset their babies. It is hard to see what
Influenza viruses do for each other, compared with what they do for you
And me. Tapeworms counteract mammalian obesity, but not on purpose
Surely? Altruism is a rare blossom on Planet Blue. But has it not evolved?
Primitive in form, and if humans never did it very well, at least we tried.

Triple Beings

Mad Mother Nature has made myriads of monsters
In her time: so it's our turn to play her Gaian tricks.
We'll do our best and worst with her and if she were
A conscious being she'd be astounded by our versatility.
Dying as a species we will make new species, many with
A Frankensteinian blend of human, animal and I.T., it
Of the cyber-persuasion, a triple being, a new divine trinity
Saving H. Sapiens per se is hopeless, but not-per se is easy.
All of science is here, technology still comes, plus our will,
In ten years or less there will walk the triple beings, intelligent
Resourceful, moral, hard to kill, self-servicing, not self-serving,
Co-operative geniuses of metal, man and other beings

Treasure Trove

I am there in spirit, soul even I suppose, on this planetary paper, here and there
For you, for me, in our enduring crisis. I cannot live for you or you for me, for
Two, whatever the song says, cannot live as one nor without either, nor even I
For me, or you for thee, whoever you may be, everyman and every lady before
His and her unmade maker. What is the crisis? I hear the indifferent chorus chant:
Greeks in love with rhetoric and mystery, though killing questioners on principle;
Romans enjoying our disembowelment in the grateful dust; Augustinian cant
Surfing the centuries until the Cartesian virus and Newtonian cooking apples
Brought us to divine doubt; yes, what crisis is it that merely eats uncertainty?

The Mystery of Grace

The crisis grows, though, like the horde of terracotta statues, staring at nothing in
The absence of their emperor, the dead, gone, never-was god-man of their dreams
Like the selves of ourselves, lining the walls of our inner voids, clamouring to be
Like, or liked by, gods, or any god, or the god, or any paregoric, something for the
Pain oh everlasting empyrean GP, we godless outcasts in this unpromising land.
Does God play gooseberry to our loving and our dying like a distant relative?
The tribes have different opinions, some none at all, some killing like and unlike
With equal enthusiasm. Not you and I, and our many selves, surely not, we live
A decision already taken in an uncertain heaven: our gods are only human, with
Paranormal tentacles, like giant squids inky in the blackness of the deeps.
Does it seem more than this? Has the cosmic story only just begun? Too soon
To tell? The human tragi-comedy is either nearly over or just a noisy overture
To mighty things ahead. We do not know how to know or not to know for sure
Any future, the pasts are arguable, the present almost ungraspable, and gods
Still seduce us as we brave it out, and these selves of ours are sirens on the rocks.
We listen to our siren selves, their songs of fear and comfort, hating evanescence.
But closing ears to false cadences we can often sense the presence of a presence,
On the liminal edge of mind, and at our peril we may trap it, calling it the essence.
There is no shame in ignorance where knowledge has no place,
Nor is there any reason to refuse the utter mystery of grace.

I Think, Therefore . . .

Our old friend, René, birthed himself again out in the stars
And so many of us followed, feeling newly freed from doubt,
As mind surveyed the material clay and knew itself unique:
Body was for bidding, spirit reigned in heaven and on earth.

A perfect world, Cartesian paradise: a pity it was flawed
By the unconsidered question: the location of the watcher.
A void is a void is a void: something or nothing, nought
Equals nought not one or a million million million plus.

Where then am I present, or you, or anyone, on or in or
Outside the mortal coil? The first reality seems real enough
For everything to be, except everything I imagine that I need
To hold together a gossamer solidity which seems beyond.

I have not yet learned how live in the other place, a land
Well known to a thousand poets and prophets, which does
Not make it real, although it takes hold of my errant senses
And they unbelieve themselves, or take a sceptic's stand.

If it were possible to steer clear of gods and devils, detour
Around a hundred delusions, five hundred damnable dogmas,
I might yet come cleanly into the second space, here on earth;
Yet nowhere, not even a location, more a state, like air or water.

Farewell Humanity

To open the discussion - a conversation in a vacuum glass
If ever there was one, is it not so? - I ask: How can any
Of us know to what, to whom, to where, to turn, for truth
When human subjectivity is all we have about us. Try, then,
To ask a man or woman, if you dare; and what do you expect?
They must tell you what is best on earth, the finest qualities and
What will they say, what on earth can they reply? So, modestly,
He could tell you that good men, even better men than he exist;
Conceivably, she might point her fingernail at nicer types than she;
They could go for instead of us in general? Is there any praise to sing
For dog, or camel, tree, or snake, or even animals cetaceous,
If we know we're only opting for something to replace us?

We'll Make God

We'll thrust evolution forward in an epic leap, we'll make God
At last, with all the virtues, and few, if any, of the vices,
We'll perpetuate something of ourselves and of our fellow brutes
And something of our perfect machines, not as robots, not as slaves,
Nor marauders nor crusaders, but keepers of the faith in mind and ethic
They'll be more than their components, more than we could ever be
At last the empty myth of god or angel will become beautifully real
And if there had been a divine creator this would be its dream come true.
There's more to this than meets the mind. We'll create a cosmic purpose
The triple being will build transcendent soul-mind, step by step
Chardin's feeble hope becomes a giant certainty, the trinal being
Will itself evolve, not a Darwinian struggle, but a path of destiny.

Ancestral Home

I longed for perfect peace, in a timeless, slowly busy place
Where all exists and nothing happens, where I could face
My daimon down, embrace him, show him pain and paradise
As they fill me, tell him my delicious troubles, cast the dice
Among the tall grasses and yellow cups, lose the spotted cubes
Down in the secret water where bullheads charge and the tubes
Of Juncus spear upwards to the filtered sun.
With sweet indifference, no friend of mine, nature runs across
My track. Its self-absorption calms my fever, a gift of blissful loss.
They come towards me, the ancestors, murmuring in green shadow;
I think they live here, like willows and kingcups, spirits that endow
A different detachment, how ends mean less than nothing, whether
From back, or front, and how I slip and sail about as if a feather
Falling from the breast of the migrating swan.

Flowing Silt

Now it clears. Life flows through us, not us through it: we are the beds
Of small streams, broad rivers, even of the moving seas, our identity
Exists like particles of clay and sand, washing in the current, material
Yet immaterial, evanescent information, swept by fins of ghostly fish.
What path then, for me, or my kin, what intention moves this sediment?
Mind moves across the silty bed of my pretended purpose, mind more
Than mine, perhaps a cosmic push to conscious agitation of atoms, or,
Energies of atoms, the ubiquitous, indescribable, thrust of happening:
My ancestors both near and far speak now to me, from quantum fields;
Grandfathers, grandmothers, other fathers, further mothers, all the same
Messengers of transformation, their gift of redemption to the surviving edge,
Confessors for my delusions. They hear my plea. Their silence tells more
Than memories. It is a story of unrequited passion; the loving and hating
Of earth, and those symbolic spirits in air or on the waters: humankind
Has wasted everything in manufacturing knowledge and dominion.
The Message is in the unseen print, hidden between flaring headlines, words
I barely comprehend, words that say the crown is within our fevered grasp.

Beloved Void

As I now consider how my life has been spent
I cannot remember how or when I made my intent.
'Higher purpose' seemed no purpose at all
Compared with the everyday, merciless call
Of living by numbers, working the day, endlessly urging
Myself with duty, loyalty, principle and purging.
Then came the plagues and tempests, temptation
To old habits to intensify, to get redemption
From even harder labour, deeper flagellation.
I looked to heaven for inspiration, as for a muse
To give me divine authority, my moment of power,
But she didn't turn up for my glittering hour.
Something new then came. It was beautiful. Perfect.
The exquisite form of emptiness. Silence. I reflect
Upon this Void and see its shining mystery, the joy
Of nothing to be done; even when and where I employ
Insignificant resources to counter meaningless confusion
And draw you and others to me in brotherly collusion.
What is it that wipes a hand across the gaming table
Of existence and tells me to be quiet, says the fable,
Ends this day? Am I ready to be cleansed of knowing?
To stare the cosmic whirlpool in its vacant eye, then going
Higher and higher in pure air, becoming transparent, afloat
The empty consciousness? May I lose my many-coloured coat?

The Man in the Street

We've all met him.
We've all been him.
That Man in the Street.
He is the one who has ditched us all.
Ask him his opinion and what do you get?
His opinion.
His worthless, flatulent, uncomprehending, absolute
Opinion.
In the Land of The man in the Street
The Man in the Street is King
Unless he is actually the King
In which case, he is both supreme and idiotic.
So how do we know what is what?
What is true, what is right, what is
The real McCoy?
The genuine article?
There was a time he'd say, that Man in the Street,
He'd say it was true because
He'd Read it in The Paper or seen it on The Box
But now there isn't Paper, Box or even Street
What does the Man in the Street, who isn't, do?
Ask him what happened to the world, ask him
Where it all went wrong, ask him to write history.
If you dare, if you can find the imposter, ask
For an explanation for his action and inaction
And he will tell you, or would if he could, barefaced
Mega-lies about greedy bosses and grub-politics
Forgetting his own complicity.

Ask a Stupid Question

I, like Anfortas, immobilised, yet unresting, my tribe heavily
Unredeemed, futile kings, yet blessings-rich, grail-blazoned,
I ask salvation, a miraculous confection, nothing less than why
Do I linger here? Can I not die with honour upon a bloodstained
Cloth of Gold, as was avowed when baptised noble murderer?
As warriors are. All men are heroes. Born to war, to rest in peace.
I pursued my enemy. His name was Ignorance. I ran him through.
Yet he wounded me. He filled my veins with poison. The toxin, doubt.
I do not believe the old stories. Nor the new. I am distrust its very self.
But my angels plague me. They bother me with wonders made of paper
And pretty paint and the wings fall from their backs, their haloes crack,
And they plunge into the sea like old Icarus. Now I must turn
Upon myself and ask the question that seemed too impractical for a king,
'In the Fourth Reality is everything the same?' There is a great silence.
Everything the same? Everything cannot answer a part of itself. Prayers
Cannot exist. Everything speaks only to itself . . . .
It dawns.Upon itself. The Three Realities cannot be. My mistake. Each
Includes the others and itself and all are also in the Fourth. All is actually
One. As has been said before. Though no-one has believed it. Sounds good.
A mantra for all seasons. But, oh, but, what if it is literally the basic fact
Of all existence? No exceptions anywhere. Sects and insects are identical
Like norms and worms, gods and dogs, you and me and her and him
And the earth below and air above, all and every one is all and everyone.
And everything is here for ever, somewhere, somehow, one totality.

Border Crossings

They are the ones I sought
Unrealising my seeking:
The ones my soul has caught
But not within its keeping.
Who these are? Who goes there?
The unperemptory guide, the cool star,
The quiet insistence
Inside and outside, up and down,
Outermost, innermost,
Uppermost, deepest:
Who are these? What there goes?
I can look through their eyes,
Confess and claim the loving:
These ones have found me, brought
Me to my border crossings.
How to cross? What travel rights?
The rites of passage are mine and only
Single ticket, window seat
Seeing highest, seeing farthest;
Who can pilot? What navigates?
I hesitate to speak my needs
Uncertain of their way of coming,
They who stand so close to me
With intimate and distant seeing
Risk everything. Save everything.

I learn a distance to be held, close
Together,
I teach a nearness and a farness, both
Unlimited.
Who can cross? What bounds us?
Though they are the ones I sought,
And now I realise my seeking,
Though they are within my keeping, they are:
Here and there. Not anywhere. But everywhere. They
Are fixed and everchanging: we join together
In mutual separation, connected, bonded, freewheeling
I ask, and give, Nothing and Everything.
All is true. Suffice it to say.

Ode to Pervasive Development Disorder

Ironic, iconic, ionic, bionic, demonic:

Bipedal life on earth, endemic dysfunctionality.

Pervasive equals Extensive; development equals Evolution;

Disorder equals Confusion;

This is us, people, everywhere, since we started, preolithic.

We have Extensive Evolution Confusion, EVC,

In all directions at once, ever since we

Opposed thumbs and walked arse-down.

There's a name for it, not merely acronymic,

A real disease: until the seeds of doubt are sown:

Asperger's Syndrome? Sprinkler's Disease?

(Psalm 51: 'Asperges me, Domine, hyssopo et mundabor'.)

But no, all wrong, you'd be all wrong to think

That we have rumbled ourselves; it's them we mean,

As HFAs (High Functioning Autistics);

Which was also all wrong

Try schizophrenia? No, wrong too, too wrong.

First identified, wrongly, in 1944

Diagnostic categorised DSM IV in 1994

Fifty years of EEC (Extensive Evolution Confusion)

When all the time, them was us, we've all got it;

More or less, which is why we're down the pan.,

All people that on earth have dwelt are in DSM IV

Diagnostic and Statistical

Manual of Mental Disorders:

It's a mad, sad, bad, damn, world (of madmankind)
Ogod knows it's them not us, the troubled ones
Who try to run away from us into themselves:
Pull the other one, it tinkles,
And sprinkles.
Holy Water!

Sacred Songs

Samain Circus

The year started before it had begun, with acts
Upon the high wire I could have done without
If asked, as I was not as far as I was aware. Not
Aware enough, it would seem, to see death and
Despair and revelation and loss heaving over the
Horizon, making openings and closures, acrobat
I'm not, now, if I ever was, and up there down I fell
And landed unsafely on cold hard clinical pads in
Wards unlovely and unloved. Samain welcomed
Me to spaces between worlds, tricked, treated, all
Hallows broke loose, swept me up, spat me out
From the cosmic vacuum-cleaner to find a dead
Sister, a wounded wife and a fine-shredded self
Speculating on evolutionary questions. Such as
How did I get all the way here from way back then
When I was a scented violet on a sunny bank by
The road to paradise with no motor cars, yet, and
A sister arriving any minute, the first one that I'd had,
Who saw the world and only stayed to say goodbye
A ten-day life and a soft pad in a country graveyard,
That's what she got for all my mother's trouble and I
Wept and cursed the slow-worm sliding by her grave
I was too young for zoology, the wisdom of it escaped
My grasp, the wisdom of the serpent in the churchyard,

What wisdom? But I was too young for wisdom, too,
That was still to come. Just in time for my second lost
Sister, who tried to die an infant and was saved to die
When I'd become a wise old moron, when it would
Hurt most, worse than the petulance of that viola child.
No praise for the rage that comes with age, no sage
Recompense; therefore I ask what can the old man do?
Reconsider the idle lily in the field? Count his ribs? Take
To Ovaltine? Dye my hair white? Take a walk to the edge?
Ah, the Edge! Where The Fool steps out. Oh, *That* Edge!

Love Bites

Love is all, most of us agree, all of us think maybe at least
It could be everything that counts. So let's say that's true.
But one says 'where does the pain go?' 'Into the love, where
Else?' Of course. 'No, no!' she says, 'it must lie among the
Roses. Pain will soften, down among the roses. Flowers
Especially with thorns, can take a tragedy away from me.'
She wants disappointment to keep away from love, that
Joy must be untarnished: let the roses cope, stabbing it
To death if there's no other way. Or let disappointment
Kill the roses, either way is okay so long as love does not
Suffer the throes of misery. There is silence in the court
Of King Sympathy, while he ruminates upon his Queen.
He has thought. He will speak. She will hear.
'My dear Lady of the Lake, listen to my enlightening.
I say to you that pain and love are the soul of congruence
Or, to put it plainly, you must suffer with the love else
That love is an unlovely lie.' The court observed her.
It, they, saw she was discountenanced, the King was
Not inclined to unenlighten his mind, so bright it shone.
Knights and ladies murmured in distress, to see the royal
Couple in dispute. And looking deep into their noble
Hearts they felt their own uncertain judgements upon
The issue dividing the royal realm. Did love conquer as it
Should? Or was it an illusion? Was not suffering the thing?
A Wise One whispered, 'The true passion is in the roses'.

Connected Items

You might almost call it a haberdashery store - Life:
A mass of unconsidered trifles, buttons, ribbons, silks
Cottons, socks, napkins, handkerchiefs to weep into, and
Everything else of small but vital significance, like blood
Corpuscles and leucocytes and mitochondria not to mention
The bloody everlasting genes. Life's blood, this mess
Of things, which simple-minded geniuses try to convert
To comprehensive, comprehensible, packages of unitary
Theory. By all means make a Theory of Everything, so
Long as it leaves no detail unturned. Otherwise a pox
On single, mind-bent disciplines. The investigation is
Vacuous that disregards the all, an all that must be greeted
With open-minded arms, relevance cherished, somehow,
Anyhow, making all connections with everything, for all
Is everywhere you look, see the connections sprout before
Your goggled eyes. Assemble the joints and tendons
Of life's skeleton and carcase, a post mortem in reverse,
For knowledge of any worth is necessarily piecemeal, with
Quantum squabbles everywhere at once, billions in the
Same place. Why should life be simple or made to seem
So, making it hardly worth the living, or the dying, often.

Ante-Hero

His worst sin was believing in his own bad self-publicity.
How was that allowed to be? How can a youth be callow
Enough to set out for the stars, yet see his flights of fancy
Through a prism of self-reproach? Who told him he was garbage
Despite manifest talent? Who made him feel sub-optimum
As he rose above the herd, as he drove himself to win the
Battles he had not started? Perhaps he recognised his lusts
As poisons, his aspirations as the arrogance of a peasant,
His rage the self destruction of a boy-man before his time.
He would live as he began: despite the winning he would
Always lose, Pyrrhic to his core. Yet that dream would last him
Till the end, maybe further than the end, that dream of loveliness.
Who gave him that revelation? Who made him a sacred sinner,
A tear-stained struggler after comprehension, love, or truth.
He could see it as miraculous if he could see anything in the
Blind acceptance of futility. It was always life well lived
However he might drag down his own credentials. One day
He might yet, in age, recognise the true brilliance of that youth.

Cynics

He, she, they, all; cynics, notwithstanding their extremity
Of self-absorption, desired with everlasting lust, *Magic*.
Not prestidigitation, not rabbits out of hats by their ears,
No, not that, not pretence paraded for children to goggle
And giggle, or for credulous seekers for thrills. No, none
Of that, for certain sure. Our cynics are hunting for meat.
To eat, with a knowing wince, and a rheumy eye, the miracle
They know to be impossible, the flesh of the wild chimera,
The cynic's cynosure. But not merely minor ursa, even if a
Starry little bruin made of stars, nor any astrological hum
Bug or not, as taste decides, no, the food of the nihilist must
Be copper-bottomed genuine, double-blinded by experiment,
Ambrosia, no less, by appointment to Zeus and Yahweh and
Every myth from the big bang onwards, eat the caviare and
Never mind the sluggish, innocent beluga, dead upon her
Emptied fifty fathomed bed. Can it be quite as bad as that
On the range where the sceptical buffalo roam, hiding and
Seeking their Indian gods? Why not? The sceptical question
Covers all exits, and entrances, like a bouncing squid, ink
Spilt everywhere, as cheap as blood, as life runneth over
The jay-walking magpie searching for prizes that glitter.
Magic, then, *magic,* by all means, available to the hunter
That takes it as it comes, like a non-discriminatory Feirefiz,
The black-and-white conqueror who's none too fussy which

Divinity is behind (if anywhere,) everything, so long as he
Gets the golden girl, the bearer of the holy grail, and
Takes her to his converted kosher couch as if she were real.
What do the hemispheres of arrogance, the brains of clerics
And atom-splitters and bisectors of a hair, what do the
Porage oats in the skull know of magic? What licence do
They hold to kill either known or unknown truths or lies
When nothing, the cynic's golden negative, is empty of sin
And virtue, a void full of anisotropic directions. The cynic
Then, must eat his top-hat and let the rabbits run free-range
In the dewy grass; the nihilist is saviour of everybody's
Sanity but his own, it is the service he brings to earth like
The fool Prometheus. Serves him right if the magpie gets
His humbles, bringing the titan to his wit's conclusions.

Clappybabbypsychohappy

Clappy

If you are in doubt regarding the actual substantive nature of sanity
Join a group, community or congregation, any collection if you like
To be unalone, join and enjoy, open up your being to the Energy or
Lord, or Universe, or any sub-division of the Search for Whodom or
Better still a charismatic personage on another planetary resonance.
But do not think it's free of charge - that lunch is astronomically
Expensive, even if it's only bread and wine or tofu crispy nibbles,
And most of all, there will be the question nobody ever answered:
'How much of this, like life anyway, is remotely near reality?' To
See the madness in yourself first learn to enjoy it in all the others.

Babby

But first, you must learn to recognise it, otherwise how to tell?
You may think yourself an atheist, perhaps, the mad quintessence in
The iron grip of dismissive certainty. It is a lonely pinnacle of pain.
Just think about the insanity you clutch unto your cold breast
And ask the lethal question, 'Am I really, truly sure I am just a
Pointless accident?' In other words, are you madly, truly, free
Of all intention and completely convinced that anything can happen
To you without any purpose whatsoever. If so, why are you here?
Why aren't you drunk in a ditch, or dangling on a rope, or giggling
Happily in the lotus-laden atmosphere of endless hopeless ecstasy.

Psycho

All atheists are insane, but not all madmen are atheists. This group
Of yours harbours other representative lunacies, a miniscule sample
Of those in the world, your little coterie has seven of the insanities:
One is the traveller in time, a Pharaoh, an Aristotle, an Abraham;
Two is the death-survivor of tomorrow, too wonderful to disappear;
Three is the syncretic Christian, making and having his own way;
Four is the shaman, the traveller in earth and fire, unscathed crazy,
Five is the heavenly healer, one-way goodness from her every pore,
Six is the rebel, proud defender of his dystopic, rose-red battlefield,
Seven is the believer in unbelief, atop his topsy-turvy underworld.

Happy

And that is one small clique of intending kindred spirits joined in
Their stated aspiration, separated by jealousy, weeping, hugging,
Promising earth and heaven as if theirs to give, joined in pity, like
The curate's egg, addled but optimistic, pledging life-supporting
Love upon demand, or even without being asked, is not this bliss?
Well, come to think of it, if six billion could do it, maybe we'd be
Better for it, and kinder to the beasts and trees and flowers, maybe.
Bury our beliefs, then, and concentrate on undoctrinal kindness?
Oh, I wish, but do not hope. Yet there is the clique. Seven souls
Entwine, imperfect, even ratty, but hands hold me, eyes smile.

Deep-frozen

There in the hinterland is a field of ice
And absolutely void of life, nothing lies
Beneath the solid sheet, nothing stands
Upon the crystal lake of desiccated blood.
That is where my grief lies, like a fly
In amber, frozen resin, a mindless insect
Screaming like an amplified mosquito, my
Dead live there: waxworked and perfect
Replicas of a dream that died recurrently
Died in the ice, crushed by the glacier
They are nothing in a nothing field of ice.
That emptiness is the overwhelming adversary
But also the undeniable reality denied in
Loving, anxious eyes, and death waits at the
Entrance to the frozen land, the faultless
Protagonist, the doorkeeper of a freedom
Which only enslaves the ones that are left
Alive, unfrozen bodies animated and alarmed.
I had two sisters, who take me to the frozen
Land. They are specific guides and guardians.
Of the many in amber, they are most elusive
And yet defined in sharp awareness, needles
In the haystack of my mind, more piercing
Than the shattering by greater, heavier loves

Hoxination

When I was seventeen, I was enamoured of logos and of bio
In equal measure, but could see no decent wage or openings
In the ancient craft of nature study and it was even irksome
At school, with leaf and bud collections, labelled on a trestle,
Maybe it would have been different had I heard of Gilbert White.
As it was, I took off myself to Birmingham, Edgbaston, and sat
At the feet of giants, as I saw them, and the biggest of them all
Was Professor Peter Medawar, Green Man, God of Embryology.
To my surprise, I found him unomniscient, though now I know
Everybody is. Even him. And what was his heel of fair Achilles?
He could not tell why identically talented cells became different
Geniuses, specialising in this or that, as if born to their destiny
Which, clearly, they were not, having exactly the same genetics
As each other. I thought about it until I saw the lovely truth,
Now a comfort in my dotage, that science was always just as
Wrong or incomplete as any of the religions that I had discarded
Before the age of ten. And so I found a freedom of the mind, long
Before it reached my heart and (shall I call it) soul, and in a way
Became a naturalist at least in spirit. As for embryology and even
More for Darwinistic tendencies, I remained a conditional believer.
But now, today, sixty years on, long post-Crick/Watson, when
Officious lunatics want schoolchildren to be taught the Genesis
Myth as fact, a revelation comes in the pages of the New York
Review of Books, May 2006, saying 'Evolving Evolution' and

It has the bits that Medawar could not have had, as they had not
Been uncovered then, the wonderful world of the Proteins of Hox.
It's a story too long for a short poem, a subject too labyrinthine
For simple prosody, yet the bottom line is another footnote to
The history of ignorance and faith: the majestic magic of the gene.
Of all the creatures and the vegetables that on the earth do dwell
The gene reigns supreme in that it lives in every living thing and
Among the genes are hoxes that manage all the rest into forms
And anatomies, the super genes that run the show in segments
Or in tools and organs, switching on and off and saying what
Goes where and when, supervisors in an assembly-line creating
You, or me, or earthworm, bacterium, toadstool, orangutan.
These hox switchers are few and far between, as foremen should be;
I, human, have four octets of them, and my hundred trillion cells all
Told what to do by the thirty two, who were once instructed in *their*
Duties by my dear mother's hormones when I was a mere egg in
The living cup under her apron. Evolution, then, what of that?
Quite a lot, in fact, and faster than we thought, though nowhere
Near a fundamentalist's week. Not only do the hoxes push the cells
Along, but capillaries search for opportunities to spread oxygen
Around and breed new tissues, an enzyme sniffs out new food. As
If, then, the random changes also have intent entwined. A human
Might be reassembled from parts of its simian prototype in a mere
Five hundred thousand of years, a blink of the geological eye-lid.
The boy-naturalist inside me knows there's more to come and that
It won't please everyone; why should it? Nature hasn't finished with

Us, or itself. Not yet. All creatures and vegetables who on earth do
Dwell have a million million catastrophes ahead and not all of them
Will be beautiful experiences. The hox genes have the matter up their
Proteinaceous sleeves and there's nothing much we can teach them.
So forget your troubles, think long-term, evolution will outlive you
As you well know. Or if you don't, your descendants will, when
The genic hoxes come around in their octets of initiation boxes.

Savant

I know what big and lovely silver planes are supposed to mean
In dreams. Adventure; self-inflation; erotomania; desire to get
A life, away from this life, that is, and to a high life, somewhere.
So, hardly aware it was a muggy morning in grey, soaked, city,
I clung to my bedsheets as I watched the giant, fat, torpedo, with
Wings, graze the roof and its tail fin hit a chimney and airbus
Settled on the house with relief and the walls stayed standing.
And I thought about the insurance rather than anything more
Personal except I wondered how the passengers were getting on
Or off and how my neighbours must be wondering, not knowing
It was a dream. And when I'd shaken off the Boeing from my
House and consciousness, I saw another vision, from yesterday,
And another meaning, because big shapes have been this way
Before, above my head, hanging in the air or shifting at speed
Or being gigantic mountains topped with snow, and even
Grounded spaceships in the fields of home. Then another thought,
Bigger than all the rest, intruded its surprising presence: that
Semi-being, the one behind the arras of the lady's mind, was
Pretty well ubiquitous, keeping up a stream of information that
Takes the mind in a thousand forms, causing confusion and
Minefields of explosive certainties and a great deal worse.
But, I thought, it is also the grail, the cornucopia, the holy word.
What is going on? What *has been* going on, all these centuries, I
Queried, prosaically. The name that comes to mind, at the head

Of a long queue, is Thoth, also known, by some, as Hermes, Thrice
Greatest, Trismegistos, the first of all the 'Seths', the 'Don Juans',
The 'Merlins', the prophets and messiahs and saviours of our
Misbegotten race. Thousands of them, stretching out in a line
Back to eternity. This gigantic nexus, I thought, includes poets,
Philosophers, mystics, teachers, doctors, and not least of all
Lovers, mothers, fathers, actors, and comedians. Not all, not
Every grain of sentient sand can be a pearl, and some are grit
In the ointment, poison in the ambrosia. And then there's the
'Need to Understand' or to make liquid gold freeze into bullets.
Poor Neanderthal didn't make it. Not enough poets, perhaps.
Or too many humans elbowing away. We don't seem to know
How to listen to our call, even after five or twenty thousand
Years of hearing it in the swirling wind of the desert and the
Pines, the call continues in a million voices, often agonised by
The endless savagery of man, sometimes singing a melody
Of grace, a song uncorrupted by the will to conquer or convert.
Chance, or not chance, has made me see the truth that dogged
My precious doubt, as if to put it in jeopardy. Too many burnings
And beheadings in my buried consciousness had made me fear
My own perceptions, and the enlightenment that stalked me.
It is late, but probably just in time, to set aside the Gods and
Devils and the Faithful and the Damned, and all the fury I have
Felt, not realising that this living death was made by man and
Compounded by blind nature; not realising I could walk in my
Own light, careless of the hardened eyes of certainty on every

Side. In some sense, I have always been, an impersonal being,
An atom in the nexus of human consciousness, and maybe more,
Though that is beyond consideration or even interest. We are
Still many, those who know the taste and smell of grace, won
By diligent innocence, and borne upon the loving of each other
Without possession, presumption, or the double-dealing mind
Of the sanctimonious exploiter of our moment in the sun. And
Now, maybe, the monster on my roof might fly off into history.

Paraclete

We met in the top corner of the field, by the dynamic old works
Where our fathers had been fashioned and our roots docked
And I gave them speech saying: 'This is the path of life and light
Which we can take together; are you coming with me on this day?'
They nodded indolently and my cells knew I was in trouble with
Them but I had faith to go on. The power was in me and I had no
Choice but to blunder on, offering them shared ownership of
Soul beauty, ready to offer itself to us if we could accept it, at
All and ultimately entirely. I stood there in the sun, listening to
The wheels churning the aerial messages, feeling the ineffable
Strength inside me. I was full of grace. Grace embraced me. Not
Me alone, not just for me, this was power for ever, all-embracing
There in the sun by the old dynamic factory of our guilt and our
Inertia, about to move diagonally across the great, green space
Towards ourselves, if we could wait for ourselves to catch up.
Time was short as well as endless and I tried to hurry them into
Their own beauty but, just as we might have stepped into the air
One said she needed the lavatory, then another had to go shopping
And a third said her career was at stake with this strangeness; then
A fourth worried that her husband might disapprove. They all
Scurried off and I stood in my glowing majesty, connected to the
Cosmos, a failure, all lost, what use was I in my bloody glory?
One was left. She moved towards me, held my hand, kissed my
Damp, damned, cheek and said 'I am Grace', and then she stepped
Into me, fusing to my bones and brain, and I fell to my creaking
Knees and slowly sank into the warm old earth, saved by grace.

Octet

In the next room there is a woodwind,
A woodwind, oh what a word it is!
And it is a woodwind octet, playing:
Boccherini, is it? Or maybe Haydn, who can
Tell? They are making a sound of spirit, no
Less. In this room, where I am listening, there
Is another octet, the same, without woodwinds,
Listening; so two octets. A set of sixteen.
The music ends.
But one plays on.
Not composed this way, evidently, a sort
Of musical error-crime is being made. I know
The girl and her instrument. She goes on,
And on, making a silence around her by her
Magical mistake or sorceress's intention.
Her solo ends. Real silence rains upon me.
I am Ariel, freed from the mad, malign master.
No more Prospero, no, never, and I laugh.
Now the silence rains about me. I am the
Maverick, now, my laughter is a lone line
Of disharmony. I say my Ariel's truth:
That single melody made the world whole.
No-one saw the joke or loved the miracle.
Why? Well, no-one else heard her solo song.

I was as bad as she was, laughing to a score
That never was. How could they not hear?
That music still,
Still plays,
In Ariel's head.
Prospero is dead.
Music to ears
Of the living.

Speak to me of Ecstasy

How can I speak with
Words that do not yet if ever they will exist among
The bricabrac that piles up in cobwebbed corners
Of my still to be uncovered secret consciousness?
I think of that first seen Orchis mascula, Early Purple
Genius of the grassy hill where my youth marched
In search of barely remembered or imagined bliss,
And there and then it happened, that it was ecstasy
I do know undisputedly. But I cannot speak it so
That it has dimensions, a measured experience it
Will not allow itself to be and I am dumb about a
Thing that counts above the all and every ordinary
Language that I am told will show me what I am.

Hermes' Orders

In the dark and fast asleep I killed them all
in death-rampage-dream, cold and unattached, freeing
my unsleeping but asleep self from every piece of past.
With me now is the memory of broken, bloodied, bodies
and the uncertainty of their innocence or guilt, although
I know that they were only inner images of my own burdened
being, and that they were ripe for ritual slaughter. Yet I still,
grieve for them after nurturing them for unknown eons.
Even now, in the light of rainy day, I feel the steel of the
automatic, with life and death of its own as it leapt
ravenously at my old friends and enemies.
Then, free, I walked and ran in a new-born landscape,
There were others free with me, numinous but blank.
I left them to explore my new world, a new dreamscape.
There was grass. There were trees. And sky and water.
And a path. I needed birds, squirrels, any living thing, to
populate my new world. But it was empty, if not dead.
Then human voices. The words were meaningless. The men
were ill-disposed, if not dangerously inclined and I ran
from them, still free, not desolate, not hopeful, a mere
visitor in a foreign land where no interest showed itself
and I was starting from nothing. I woke to knowledge.
Thoth's law: I was bound to transmutation, he decreed.
And here it was: a blank cheque and no apparent bank
to pay out my Trismegistos winnings. I may be free;
but where's the lunch? I must dig a hole for water? I must
find berries and chew bark? I will sleep inside a holly bush.

Shadow-Speak

I have half-believed the story;
That one about the shadow, suppressed in the sub-conscious
Those feelings that no-one wants to
Own up to; bad thoughts; ill-intentions best left out of account,
That come up and hit you when
You're down: proving they actually exist - that story.
It happened last evening, to me,
Not the first time, either, but rarely so certainly so,
I said something very silly, and
Didn't know where it came from - but, obviously, I know.
I said, 'I don't like old women',
And felt a fool, which I was and am, to say such a damned stupid
Thing, but it's true. I do dislike
Women - and men - who are older than me, that is eighty-plus,
Because they are like me - and more than
That, worse, because they are nearer the bloody end. And worse,
They, old women, eighty-plus women,
And eighty-plus men, are beautiful. I can't bear to think of them.
Gone. And mostly me, my dearest self
Seeing that reality and feeling that going and being afraid and
Saying that I'm not.
Then she, who is my most loved, that damned woman is a whole
Year older than me; so how could
I like her, down in my mad shadow? How could I say it, then, that
Stupid sentence? How could I
Not?

Evening Music

Spectral Initiation

Eight hundred square inches of
White wood pulp, brilliantly blank,
Stare, vertical or flat, threatening
Unco-operation, indifferent, as is
White's wont. It won't love me back
So dare I desecrate its virgin purity?
The teacher-man said, 'Remember, class,
This rectangle of nullity is all yours - do
Anything you like, just cover that bloody
Whiteness, it hurts your eyes'. Not true:
It hurts my pride; I cannot improve on
Perfect whiteness: I am white-bound.
I have colours: oily, plasticky, gouachey;
I have solvents, if no solutions, I have
Spirit, I have holy water, and detergent,
My armaments. I charge at the enemy
Gleaming whitely, insouciant, implacable
But mistaken, I have the force with me
Newton's stream of white is split by brush
And palette-scalpel, ROY G BIV emerges,
White fights back, holding on to territory
As the pigments gorge their way across
The untouched land, making things to make
The mystic realm bloom with desperation

So this is why the white was made to die?
To make this visual jabber, this potty pie?
You're all the same, artists, layabouts, wasters
Of the undefiled unconciousness, putting
Posters on holy walls, cartoons on monuments.
Gratified by graffiti, let the colours sing.

Blue

You may wonder how you got to be
A Christian, if you are, and also me,
So here's how: basically a liberty
Was taken by mad, bad, Constantine,
Pagan overlord who tossed a Roman
Coin and so decreed it was a Trinity
For us, a monogod divisible by three.
Three Gods it is, then, and all primary.

White light, too, is a trinity, as it happens:
Red, raging, Father; Yellow, glowing, Son -
That's two, then three, with Cerulean Spirit.
Such conjuring tricks! Six and/or two threes.
Yet one or (who knows) two primary origins?
Fundamentally, though, I like blue, and Spirit.
As Yellow and Red Gods are extremely hot,
Pigments of Fauvist lunatics, creating wild,

Passionate pictures. But Blue, ah! Blue!
And which? Aforesaid Cerulean, say?
Or moody, acid, Prussian? There's Cobalt,
And sickly sweet Ultramarine, getting on
For reddy purple, too Fatherlike for me.
Prussian likes yellow and gives a green
Such as seen in vegetable allotments
With pretty lettuces and adolescent beans.

Cobalt Blue, a liberal, happy shade,
Good for anything, even sky, if you
Don't fancy Cerulean, the popular
Vote; and not forgetting Indanthrene,
For Dyes and pigments and E130, while,
Phthalocyanine, greenish, bluish, helio,
Monastral, dyes intensely; but old Indigo
Doesn't qualify as Blue, being rather Violet.

Blue, then, a godless, blessed hue.
Apposite for Spirit and why not Soul too?
I could live for Blue, despite obvious objections:
Too sublime, too conservative, too deep, too cool,
Too relaxed, healing fevered psyche overfed
With religion or its opposite. True Blue, colour
Of Paraclete and Void: Oh give me Blue, Fortuna,
Bathe me in the healing waters; Azure infinitude.

Apatura Iris

A willow in a pot, goat, sallow or just plain pussy,
Unfussy little tree, except its thirst, though I suspect
It would rather be rooted in a wood, who wouldn't?
I visit it every day, because it's by the pond,
An oasis in the garden of which I'm very fond,
Nothing changes usually, but today, a July afternoon,
I found a tiny mosque of green upon the topside of a leaf,
My pussy willow had become unique, and Islamic
So it seemed, but in a week it became more dramatic,
Turning purple; another week and it burst, a suicide-bomb,
And gave way to a little wriggler who ate its holy house.
A larva, then, but whose? The caterpillar started plain
And brown, but after instars and a winter hibernation
In the fork of a sallow twig, it was one year old, and fat
Fully grown, coloured green, with striped and cream diagonals
Dark-edged, a pointed tail, two red-tippd horns upon its head.
Unique. Amongst caterpillars at least. Willow was quite wasted
By its house-guest, who rested by day, chewing lazily
Beside the leaf's midrib, then wandering at night, laying
A silken trail for going home each morning to its midrib base.
I expected a caterpillar of such age to take a long pupation.
But no, a fortnight was enough in this silver-green disguise
Shaped like a willow leaf. July-first the butterfly inside
Shook itself free, pumped its wings, became an alpha male.

In ordinary light it's main distinction was wingspan, and strength:
A big beast, purposeful, direct, with a taste for honeydew
And faeces of dog or fox. He flashed deep purple in glancing rays
Of sun, and was last seen heading for an oak-tree crown
To the gang, running rings around each other, waiting for the girls.
White-striped and -spotted, he swaggered, that Purple Emperor.

All-Round Orange

Immigrating Norman, ancient French, 'Orenge',
Invaded this Old England, home of Geoluhread:
Unpoetic 'yellow-red', but ours like 'stone' and 'henge'.
This new fruit was transitory, soft as mead,
Unrhymable was orange, unbeloved by bards.
Sweeter-sounding mandarins, tangy tangerines,
Clementines, were much more on the cards,
Crazy kumquats, sailed here in oriental ships;
All good for rhyming but not superior for
Marmalade. Orange had arrived, with pips.
Such is fruit and colour. But there's loci genius
Sweet town, Arausio, home of Celtic water-deity,
Dispossessed by Rome, then by Germans heinous,
Swallowed by the Principality of Orange, a city
Became a fruitless House, Orange-Nassau, worth
Bouncing in wars, doctrinal ferment, ferocity
Against Spain: a new order struggled for birth
Until the innocent colour was made the thing
Of a new fundamentalism of Protestants and
That invasive Dutchman, Billy the Orange King.
Weak king, poor general, maybe gay, but he
Let democracy take root, good for alien Orange.
Conversely, consider the Paisley Tartar, reverend,
Ranter, mad marcher, wild rhetorician, a stain
Upon Orange. Then, further insult to our colour:
Burgess made a psychotic, clockwork, cry of pain.
Yet Orange shines still, impervious to dishonour.

Hoodie

If you journey up the road to Scottish Perth,
As I used to do, for all my long-abirding worth,
A seasoned peeping-tom of feathered birds
I'd rest my eyes on hills too exquisite for words
Or wander by a burn, or through a wood or field,
Aves everywhere, until the scene would yield
As it surely will for you, a sight to take the biscuit
A big, black, crow, wearing an ash-grey weskit
Corvus Cornix is his formal name
Alias the Hooded Crow, the very same,
As Hoodie, Scotch Crow, Grey, and Corbie
And Carrion Crow he surely canna be.
It is hard to know why he is different
But he is far from being the only variant
In the tribe of magpies, jays, and raven toughs,
Of bright-eyed jackdaws, red-billed choughs,
While in the tops of trees you hear, then look,
To giant chanting congregations of the bare-faced rook.
Quietly spectacular, the Hoodie, black and grey,
Has a reputation in the circles of the fey
For perching on the shoulder of dying Cu Chulainn
And for being sundry gods who at one time were ruling
Around the Irish Sea, whilst in the frothy Faroes,
So the folklore truly and mellifluously now goes

Maidens at Candlemas threw stones and lumps of turf
And bones, at fairies disguised as hoodies near the surf,
An ancient double-blind experiment that could not fail
To name a future husband or prove they'd never get a male.
In those happy days when Hoodies drew the line
For me; the boundary of Northern England, a sign
That I was near my spiritual home, the land of Scot,
I cared not whether Hoodies reigned on any other plot
For sure they made their nests and raised their chicks
In Caledonia, nowhere else, did the canny Hoodie fix.
It was upon the Bosphorus, full speed to Istanbul,
After sailing endless empty, birdless miles, and full
Of avian ennui I then saw him, on a preening post:
A Turkish Hoodie, was it, or had I seen a ghost?
How far was he from Scotland, I asked, with a sigh?
Oh two thousand miles nautical, as the crow doth fly.
Was there not a simpler truth, and kinder to C.corvix,
Could he have a pied-a-terre, a place to pick and mix,
His diet, and could the crow wearing a grey cardigan
Have temporary accommodation with Eurasian Man?
Embarrassed by the truth, this poor birdwatcher's shock:
Hoodie does indeed live indigenous and of Eurasian stock,
He and his weskitless cousins occupy ten million square,
Kilometres, thirty million crows, near and far, out there.
Ever since that big mistake, I look at any bird in wonder
Whatever I might think I know, they will steal my thunder.

Aurum and Argentum

1

The winning ways of Aurum, that addiction to primacy,
Palls with age, and coming last seems just as good on
A nice day, keeping off the track anyway if it rains or snows.
But I do remember the gold of childhood and, with higher
Carats, of tempestuous pubescence. The Golden Sphere shone.
And, though now imploded under its own Newtonian inertia
The memory is brilliant in my field of relativity. I am not old;
But have acquired the skill of wise comparison; no absolute
Hangs over my sunny mind and I just dwell in the golden spell
And devil take the sunny headiness of my yellow Narcissus.
I am old. But have held on to madness. Love and beauty for
Instance still romp upon the bed of my mind, there is gold
In those high transcendental hills. Joy falls like compassion
Upon my face beneath. I am twice blessed: it was and is,
I was and am. How come? O it is that winning streaking gone.
Leaving me, once a golden calf for sacrifice, now a monkey on
A golden ball and chain, bald and chattering, still a primate.
Monkey boy, seduced by his reflection, used a lifetime to recover.

Aurum and Argentum

Silver slithered in, under the door. I know exactly when. That
Moment when I came second. A golden moment. Even if I took
Time to recognise my luck. I did not know, for ages still, that
Silver heals the dementia of gold. For that, I needed to get old.
But it was a start. There were symbols, too: white hair, grey face,
Yet gold plated over them until the glory when I came second?
The silver moment, the catastrophic tilt, new joy of irrelevance,
When I first heard and saw that they no longer heard my song.
When did they stop listening? Probably from the start. 'Stand-up'
Does not know its limitations. People laugh at anything. Fame
Conquers intelligence. Idiocy is no defence. They cry so easily
In the stalls. The dance of thirty pieces against a ring of gold:
No contest, seen from the high gods. Icarus deserves to drown,
Even if birth follows the final breath; the indrawn wisdom, ashes
Turned to isotopes unimaginable, half-lives lasting to eternity.
Silver smiles as gold medals fox-trot their stuff, sublime in perfect
Ignorance, they only know enough to know they are incomparable.
Their silver moment yet to come, freed from need to be adorable.

The Perils of Neoteny

You speak of ages of man; of what especially do you speak?
Is it man in the womb, in the cradle, or is it man the weak?
Is it man of the species, the race, is it everyman you seek?
Or is it perfection, the imago, or maturity man at the peak?
Do not believe the Avon Bard, but take that desolate septet   ;
Baby, child, lover, soldier, justice, pantaloon, and corpse-to-let;
And cast it to the landfill site, for this joyless scene, though set,
In common view, is but flawed, a delusion we must all regret.
Rosy hope is also inadvisable: a human-mind is not made for this.
Addressing an over-tragic case, sweetening it with contrived bliss,
Unable to see the simplest of truths. Dismiss all cloying artifice.
Stoical and realist, we can enter the emptiness, ending with a kiss?
No tragedy in this at all. We are only half-completed in this nursery.
We are consumed with age, not gathering the fruit of our maturity.
All and each are lost in the myth of childhood, and frozen in neoteny.
While recapitulation of phylogeny is just a lazy myth of old biology.
What is the truth of ages? It is little more than minor stages.
The arc of a human life is personally important, as our rages,
Against our small predicaments, but these are just the wages
Of useless effort, the defence of self in a billion billion pages.
We are creatures bred by earth and of little intrinsic worth,
The same as any other large or little beast, a common birth
Connects us; the ash tree of evolution hangs us from its girth
And if the gods existed we would provide them endless mirth.

Age is a consideration, not the usual fable, but a bleaker tale.
Neotenous we remain from birth to death, nearly all of us fail
To outgrow infancy, while true, deep, reality makes us quail.
The ages of man are one, so far, all for one and nearly none for all.

I Woke Up This Morning

Once again, the day was there to greet me, a friend
He seemed, as if he cared that I was still around.
But mornings, and afternoons to some degree, tell lies.
It is illusion to suppose, as I do, that something counts
For something. I was not born for anything. I happened
On a cold day in winter, I happened, when I was no age.
Unless you count nine months going through the animal
Alphabet, from fish to frog to lizard (or to bird) to ape then
Helpless, incontinent, wordless, disabled, milksucking me.
Then this morning said 'hello', today, and it looked happier
Than most I'd met, and made me wonder if this was a new
Standard of untruth among the plotting days. I am old
'Tis true, and I am quite resigned to unmerciful oblivion,
Yet what is this insistent tick of happiness upon the clock
That smirks upon my mantlepiece? Meaning left the room
Some long time ago, so what is happiness doing round my bed?
Has it not heard that old men suffer from *sans everything*?
Maybe it is the happiness disease? What! The end of the saga
Is a gas? Then it has all been for a purpose after all? Ages will
Pass and new days will dawn? But a question hangs upon the
Morning air; 'Has it all been for nothing? Really?' Apart from
This happy morning? Can I have slid along the ice of eight decades
Just to meet a cheerful day? Well easily, I suppose. Why not?
But what about what's left of me when I go? Is that age eight?

'No such thing' Resurrection, then, age five millennia? 'No, no'
Oh don't say 'come back for another go, as a goldfish'. 'No, no, no.'
Nothing then? Nought? Nil? Zilch? What have I been ageing for?
'Well, old son,' my whisper echoes, 'Some talk of soul in quiet
Places, as one born in your amiable bedroom on a cheerful day'.
This smiling morning said I could donate my soul. So here goes.

In Memory of Water

Odourless and colourless and tasteless it may be,
Yet it has the honour to be seventy percent of me.
And though the thought could drive me near insane
Water makes up nearly all my highly valued brain.
This old planet has water all over it, but mostly salty,
So the supply for seven billion people is already faulty.
Strange the way so much depends upon this simple partnership
Two hydrogens, one oxygen, atoms joined at the electronic hip.
Yet magical. Apparently this wetness has such powers: thus,
It can be solid, it can be gaseous, and even, a large plus,
Dissolves holiness within it, as in the sacred Ganges,
But be careful not to suck upon your saturated phalanges.
Best of all it has prodigious memory, reportedly recalling
Its past encounters through space and time, appalling
Simple biophysicists with its disregard for laws of nature,
A quantum particle extraordinaire, despite its tiny stature.
'Small physics' rocks the boat of Newton, it is truly worrying.
A photon can be anywhere or everywhere without hurrying.
And now there's Benveniste, a micro-scientist, don't forget,
Who suggests molecular vibration might travel on the internet
His experiments, shaking substances in water, and dilution,
Down to water only, showed (to him) a thoughtful solution.
This mindful water remembered adrenaline or nicotine, plus
Immunological signatures of viruses, which caused a fuss.

But science has itself to blame, as it invented quantum fields,
And such wild imagination unpredictably but surely yields
Even wilder thoughts, and water has become a holy grail, a source
Of miracles untold, and unexplained, that have to run their course.

Castle Stream

I see no castle, and now the stream has gone
Though Castle Stream there was when I was young;
My first water-love, gentle, shallow, crystal, all alive
With bullheads, caddis in cases, tadpoles, shrimps,
Blue damselflies above, rushes and kingcups beside,
Paradise bisected, even then, by proprietorial wire:
As I stand in memory, beyond the stream were meadows,
With trees and hills beyond, and a shining of flowers.
Behind me were the High Fields, no longer alive, hedged
Development of endless houses, the place called home
Was there, with pebbled walls, vegetables, parents, taps.
And was there once a castle, in that old territory, and did
Streams flow down from it, into small rivers and sweet wells?
I went in search of water, to those wells and rivers, until
I found the great pond two miles away, below the Bury,
The hill-fort, and knew a different paradise, at last, that
Held me in thrall through the long decade of boy's estate.
This heaven, and hell too, held me in terror and delight,
As a smallish boy, then, poaching with my rod and line,
I experimented with apprehension and hope, mirrored
By the now dark, now brilliant, green water in which
A thousand unseen fishes generally ignored me, until
The innocent deaths at and in my hands soured my zeal
Now I would become a fish. I desired immersion. Water.

Fresh or saline, snow in drifts, headfirst diving, dogpaddling.
Water is different from inside it. One day I'd have to swim.
It took long to learn that I was not built to be a fish.
Yet in pool after pool, I crawled and breast-stroked my way
Through miles of acrid and lukewarm liquid, until I stopped.
The best was yet to come. When already fairly old I found
The Tweed, a river I had always needed, at Dryburgh Abbey.
I sat by the river for three days. I came together with water.
It was the endless being that I hardly knew, the great continuum,
And I came to know it in those hours. I remember Castle Stream
But now I see that castle, stream, abbey, and river, are all in me.
Everything ends, nothing lasts, I know - except eternity.

Airily Considered

In the queasy-crazy astrologic scheme, madness of the spheres,
I, the water-carrier: oxymoronically, am also air, it so appears -
Air-marked, water-porter, singing songs within the veil of tears
Bubbling and blubbing along, to cascades of cheers and jeers.

Antiquarian, agriquarian, ancient Ariel, lord of spells and gases,
How was it on that island, lost in water, among the human asses?
How sweet the molecules of freedom, how slow the suffering passes,
How airy calls the air to air, and a phantom flock of gulls amasses.

Aquarius, man of flesh, made of water, lives on air, eats oxygen, flies,
In spaces, a wetness of lungs below, drinks his own plasma, dies
If he forgets to breathe, lies still, still lies, empty but almost wise.
Then the air is blown away, joy kissed too quickly, too lost to prize.

When air is analysed, for O, and N and C and H_2O and CO_2 and CH_4
Do they encounter molecules of soul, smells of angels; does mercy pour?
What's the point of air, or water for that matter, shouldn't there be more
For them to do, than merely fuel our monkey chatter. No heaven? No Door?

March sunlight flares, black butterfly flutters, thrush exhorts; not they,
Nor twitching squirrel, seem to share my doubts, but rather say
In every particle and way, that the briefest momentary stay
Upon this incidental planet beggars human need to pray.

This isness, and this factness of the intermediary faceless air
Tells it true: life is air, air is life, why drown them in hope's despair?
Bliss is wise, exquisite ignorance, in flimsy, knowing, underwear;
In the joy and pain of airy life, *there* soul alone is everywhere.

Disgrace of Fire

Fire is rarely sweet, with burnt soles or sweaty feet
Tearing eyes and mouth and lungs, flaying earthly being
We cannot trust its laboured breath, even as a metaphor,
Faithless fire incinerates itself, lies in our teeth, snarls
Its malevolence, delusionary satans would be its patron lords,
And imaginary gods, any God of fantasy, powerless in its embrace.
Therefore how or why could fire be praised, regarded elementarily?
Boxed in a cave or living-room it has brief usefulness, searing
Flesh of fish or beast makes Homo Carnivorens a greasy dinner,
Yet no glory there. Engines are made to fight it, red and yelling,
And engines feed on fire, one way or another. Fire eats fire.
Of all the so-called, ill-named, elements, fire is most entropic.
Water, air and earth, create as well as ruin, but fire consumes.
This greedy tyrant, a feral enemy of life, prized by pretender Zeus
Stolen by hubristic Prometheus, given to humankind as if a gift,
Of all the elemental forces it most befits us in its character:
Noisy, dirty, lethal, squandering, multiplying, suffocating, mad;
No wonder we are almost fond of it, this overwhelming evil uncle,
No wonder we warm our hands and feet upon his breath, as if friendly.
And at our end, free-thinkers choose chargrilling, not the earthy hole.

Earth-Star

1

All we on earth have this same need to live
But the animal called human must also give
Something extra to itself: WHY as well as HOW?
Bighead-biped desperately, seriously, must know
Why his kind has come upon the bluish planet
Because, he says, it cannot be an accident can it?
'Don't see why not'; say chimpanzee and mango
(Or would if they could speak our freakish lingo),
And would they care so existentially as to say
(If they could) 'Maybe you're here to teach us all to pray?'
For, so it seems, that crazy Two-Foot craves divinity
'Gods' in and out and all about, stretching to infinity

2

Not all Two-Footers, thank heavens, have this eccentricity
But even fervent untheists will trip over serendipity.
I tend to favour little godlets (or the opposite extreme,
The featureless Oversomething, a cosmic custard-cream);
So I came across a godlet yesterday, a spirit in a wood,
Not an animal, nor a plant, nor a mineral, It could
Only be a deity of The Kingdom Inbetween, a holy avatar;
Its first name is Geastrum, It is a fallen star.
I gazed upon Its radiance on the forest floor, Its seven
Pointed arms encircled a sacred mound. Its central heaven
Was raised aloft upon its columella, that far-
Flings the golden dust, a cloud above the sacred star.

3

The prodigality of old earth, making earth-star for the free,
Not just one Geastrum godlet, either, but a range of fifty.
In this genus of genius, were they designed blindly
By the desoxyribose n.a. nano-goblins unkindly
Upon earth's endless production-line, where anything goes -
'Just make it and let it rip', from dinosaur to rose:
No purpose, loveless, just making life up for the hell of it,
Godlets unlimited, or BigGod PLC, what of it?
Two-Foot doesn't like it, needs a Planner and a Plan:
Considers Geastrum in Its wood, sweetly spick and span,
Thinks big: earth IS, not HAS, a billion trillion deities,
Sees the 'plan' is no-plan, but a planet, of infinite realities.

Blood Sacrifice

I sing praises of my tribe and glorify my family:
What am I? A fool? Mindless? Automatic?
Set in stone? Lover and murderer?
It cannot be so, for am I not a living soul, human,
Even if I have a reptilian brain, and instincts of a shark,
Am I not a son of the universe, a man who's made his mark?
What mark can I have made? The mark of Cain?
Murder and rape are mainly family matters
Of the race or of the tribe or just the neighbours
When love fails and instinct or evil ride the mind's highway.
Tribe and family are more than this, the saying goes.
Prisons or havens? Both and either.
I am a victim of my kind, I suffer kinship
As do all my kind.
Trapped in primal mode, unable to grow free
Of habit and affiliation,
As a human I rebel
As a human I wish to choose
Not for me the platitudes
Of patriotism
The ropes of duty
Not, especially, the burden of belief
In queen and country, god, or martyrdom.
What then matters?
Is nothing left of natural folly?

Just the pain and glory of being free?
What more should there be?
There is more, infinitely more.
Beyond the petty binds of family and tribe
There's the cosmic connection
Being part of all that is, unfettered by an arbitrary bond.

Of Strawberries and Brambles

When it is good, family tastes like wild strawberries and cream
On a warm and sunny afternoon. There lingers too the dream
Of picking mushrooms in dew-fresh fields, and of blackberrying
In clouds of willowherb seed in a hot September, or of hurrying
By bicycle to still and watchful fishponds, in solitary blissfulness
The memory of family is full of smiling faces, and babies, and bless
My old years with sweetness, and even remembered deaths have
More than sadness, perhaps rage, but mostly images of love.

When it's bad, which is often, family entombs the minds and souls.
Parent against parent, child fighting child, all at sea, savage holes
Torn in the fabric of our being, wounds that can never fully heal,
But lie as active scars below the mind's knowing, hardly real
Yet driving the motors of our lives. Even so, why should it be otherwise?
The human animal has a fatal weakness, not afflicting other creatures:
We stay young too long, even unto death, never gaining features
Of maturity early, where family is brief, or transfers the young to tribes.

Tribe seems to be good for them, elephants, lions, apes: but not for us,
We use tribe as yet another way of suffering, Like a bad family, plus
Devious dictators, using human masses for obsessive greed and power,
While the people toil like slaves and play games like children, lower
Their eyes to kings, raise their arms to stars, and die in pointless battle.
The tribes of humankind squabble over the earth they do not own, cattle
To their overlords, sheep to themselves, the tribalism of insanity rules
In the human animal, a parody of nature, no other creatures are such fools.

Dryad

Walking in the wood one day, I thought I heard my name;
Did that tree speak, perhaps, or was someone hidden there?
Hidden indeed, a dryad in the tree, it was her mind that came
To me and I had remembered how to listen, having care
To hear a message from beyond my world, words without sound,
Sound without sound, and I knew at once the treasure I had found.
Unspoken words, no rhyme nor rhythm, but mainly drifting leaves.
This was a story too parochial, mere gossip of dryad and friend.
I asked her the unifying question, the theory of everything, to end
My quest for understanding which had exhausted me and my kind.
'It can't be trees', I said, 'not even the holy ash, not even evolution'.
'Light, she said, just cosmic light.' 'Nothing but light!', I cried:
'In the universe, is that all I'll find in nebulae, amongst the galaxies,
At the edge of space, where nothing lives? And what of life, above all?
How, in other words, did Yggdrasil cause the Big Bang, or vice versa?'
'The universe', she said, 'is just energy and energy is light. Your kind,
The blight of earth, has made its fantasy to suit its twisted mind
But purely said, there is only energy and matter is sometimes made.'
'But what of all the trees. Are they phantoms? And the earthy creatures
Are they not real at all. We can't have made them up. Just illusions?
And is the great Yggdrasil just a figment, as am I and as are you?'
'Stay with the light,' the dryad said, 'as that is what you see. You touch
And taste and hear as well, but light creates your cosmos.'
I took her truth away with me and nursed it in my soul until no more

Could I bear it rankling and corroding at the centre of my humanity
And I tried to disbelieve it as tribal pride swelled again before
I could restrain it. Even if the cosmos were merely light's serendipity
Was not human consciousness the perfect flower of evolution?
Had not the universe toiled, if mindlessly, just to make me
And the others of my ilk; could there be any other feasible solution
To that overwhelming rebus, the question why, or why not, to be?

A Trip in Triplicate

Three Journeys of Simultaneous Reincarnation

1. Ho-Hum Hero

Cotswold-bred, Midland-groomed and Yorkshire-finished, Hero

Had many a notable safari, by ship and plane and diesel train

Or cosily cocooned in the almighty executive automobile,

Yet psychically he remained in more or less one place, fixed

By oblique certainties, stuck in truth or falsity, ruled betwixt

Ambition and deep-sea blue conceit, the banality of his ilk.

Could this be called a journey? Where does it go, from, to; where?

His porage-oats of id and ego incestuously afloat in mother's milk,

Albeit liberally laced with proof libido, is such a petty majesty,

Making royal progress through his needy mind and mindy need.

This ho-hum life for ho-hum man, ho-humming klinky medals

Held to chest, pockets stuffed with certificates, degrees, tax-

Vouchers, his bottom fat and flat on board this board and that,

Bossing and being bossed, what a ho-hum warrior was this?

He battled mundane excitements, fussing as an Achilles, falling

Like Patroclus, dying like Hector, circumnavigating in Odyssean

Circles, coming home to Penelope and Ithaca a plucked chicken.

Greatness dumped upon him, Ho-Hum the archetype, blueprint

For rosy-tinted eyes, a man for all that, needs no pity, being

Heroic is all, and who is to disagree? Yet on the edge of mind

Skulks suspicion: Ho-Hum was good and great, agreed, but wasted

In war and trade and academe, was he not an Uncompleted Job?

2. Existential Marco Polo

Is there another truth, available and waiting? Could Ho-Hum become
Just-So? Could they even travel together, two of a kind, yet not quite?
How else the parade of orchids, Early Purple, Greenwing Spotted, Frog,
Greater Butterfly, Twayblade, and the deceiving Bee, all on the Hill;
Enigmatic Bird's Nest and Coralroot, among beeches down below,
Where Hero used to wander, in his Otherness, in his wilderness
Of glory, or wildly running in woods, eating nuts and berries, loving
This home, a hermit's cave, clutching books, poetry in his pocket.
He graduated severally, but Camus and Sartre held his mind in theirs:
Was this the Ho-Hum hero-man or was he the changeling, a mad elf?
Or perhaps he was rebel manque, a fraud like Marco P., ambassador,
The man who saw the Orient through Occidental eyes, played at being
The traveller from his Venetian armchair? Our Ho-Hum was gladly
Only partly house-trained, a wild dog at heart. Saved by his nature,
His sweet daemon drove his heart, he heard the charming goldfinch
Sing in groves, and understood in this other mind that he was free.
His two minds were already shorn of creeds and other fictions, no
God or monarch on his back, but neither of his brains felt or saw
The greater liberation, the freedom from himself, that invisible fly
Buzzing, dominating, his ointmented life, his existential semi-world.
A mere youth of sixty-five, he was now taken to embark, unknowing
That his ship of life was leaving harbour, heading for catastrophe.

3. Void Runner

He blamed the trauma to his frontal lobes, the thrones of Self,
Went looking for it, hoping he'd not find it, successfully failed.
He converted to conditional Druidic Zen, studied transpersonal
Sorcery, sailed on into the Sargasso Psyche, was becalmed, ill
And ill at ease, dreamed gigantic dreams, met the Giant Mountain
In his mind, discovered Essence, drowned in mystic seaweed, saw
Through the glass of Delusion, suffered the Three Poisons, hit
A welcome bottomness, down a long shaft, to silence and nought.
It was not over, nothing and everything entwined, a kind of bliss
Enfolded him, as if he'd always wanted this, leaving home at last.
The Time of the Ox had passed. That illusion of the third mind:
Mind beyond mind beyond mind, finding, catching, taming, bringing
Back the Spirit to its dwelling-place. The Soul-Journey. Completion.
Then, spirit-traveller, the spirit, the homely temple, all vanished
In a flash, to a greater nothing than any nothing he'd ever seen.
Then, the story goes, he was back in the ordinary world, changed
And unchanged, both world and traveller. He had survived passage
To and through the Void. No doubt. He could believe it. But chose
To move on to the fourth mind, or beyond, since once free why stop?
Super-Zen beckons, even if still uninvented. Once a journey starts
In earnest, why should it ever end? No need to make a meaning
Where none exists, the bliss is in the movement, go without end.

www.ingramcontent.com/pod-product-compliance
Lightning Source LLC
La Vergne TN
LVHW051839080426
835512LV00018B/2965